WHERE THE BALD EAGLES GATHER

by
DOROTHY HINSHAW PATENT

Photographs by
WILLIAM MUÑOZ

CLARION BOOKS
NEW YORK

To Riley McClelland, Leonard Young,
and all others who work to save eagles.

ACKNOWLEDGMENTS

We wish to thank Riley McClelland, Leonard Young, Jay Crenshaw, and Pat McClelland for the time, encouragement, and cooperation they gave us so generously while we worked on this book. Our thanks also go to the National Park Service for its cooperation in this project.

Photos on pages 6, 7(right), 8, 50 were taken at Northwest Trek in western Washington. Photo on page 42 was taken in western Montana. Photo on page 43 was generously provided by Harriet Allen.

Designed by Barbara Hall

Clarion Books
a Houghton Mifflin Company imprint
215 Park Avenue South, New York, NY 10003
Text copyright © 1984 by Dorothy Hinshaw Patent
Photographs copyright © 1984 by William Muñoz

Library of Congress Cataloging in Publication Data
Patent, Dorothy Hinshaw.
   Where the bald eagles gather.
   Includes index.
   Summary: Describes the annual autumn gathering of bald
eagles in Glacier National Park and examines the work of
the wildlife research project that bands the birds for
later tracking that will provide information on the habits
and life cycle of our national bird.
   1. Bald eagle—Juvenile literature.   2. Birds—Montana
—Glacier National Park—Juvenile literature.   Glacier
National Park (Mont.)—Juvenile literature.   [1. Bald
eagle;   2. Eagles.   3. Glacier National Park (Mont.)]
1. Muñoz, William, Ill.   II. Title.
QL696.F32P37   1984   598'.916   83-20852
ISBN 0-89919-230-0   PA ISBN 0-395-52598-5

WOZ   10   9   8   7   6

Endpaper photo: McDonald Creek in Glacier National Park

CONTENTS

THE MIGHTY EAGLE

The bald eagle soared over the brown winter meadow. Its yellow eyes spotted a ripple in the grass. The bird tilted its tail and banked slowly to the left. For a second it paused in the air, then plunged downward, spreading out its powerful, sharp talons just as it reached the unsuspecting jackrabbit. The eagle struck the rabbit and tightened its grip as the talons grabbed on. Then the hungry bird lifted its catch slowly from the ground and flew to a nearby tree to feed.

With its shining white head and tail and brownish black body, the large and powerful adult bald eagle cannot be mistaken for any other bird. Its wingspan can reach seven and a half feet, and its body may measure more than three feet from head to tail. The bald eagle is a superb hunter, swooping down from the skies to capture its prey on the wing.

The eagle is perfectly adapted for the hunting life. Its feet are equipped with sharp, curved talons an inch and a half long, for grasping its prey. Tiny spikes on the bottoms of its toes help grip slippery prey, such as fish. Its powerful hooked beak, which is used to tear apart food, is two inches long.

The golden eagle also lives in America. The adult golden eagle is dark brown, while young ones usually have some white on the wings and a white tail with a dark band at its tip. Bald eagles have bare legs, but the legs of golden eagles are feathered.

Eagles, along with their close relatives, the hawks, probably have the sharpest vision in the animal world. They can see a small animal, such as a rabbit or mouse, moving in the grass from a mile away. Hawks and eagles have eyes that face forward, like ours. Each eye has a slightly different field of vision, which gives the bird very good depth perception. Like us, it can judge distances very well. This is important to a hunter, which must know just when to pounce on its prey.

The two American eagles eat different food. Golden eagles hunt rabbits and large rodents like ground squirrels and prairie dogs. Bald eagles feed mostly on fish, but scientists have found that many bald eagles feed heavily on jackrabbits during the winter and will eat other food, such as dead ducks, when it is available. They have learned other interesting things about bald eagles, too. The scientists want to find out as much as they can, so they can help save this beautiful but endangered bird from extinction.

Birds are tricky to keep track of, for flight allows them to travel quickly from place to place. A favorite way to trace individual birds is for scientists to put some sort of label on them. Lightweight, brightly colored plastic tags are often used to identify individual birds. Each eagle has its own number so that the bird can be identified whenever it is seen. But tags don't help find the bird once it has flown away. In order to track large birds like eagles, radio transmitters can be attached to them. The transmitter gives out a signal that can be picked up by a receiver. Radio transmitters allow scientists to find and follow the movements of individual birds.

But how do you capture an eagle in order to attach a transmitter to it? Most of the time this would be a very difficult problem. Bald eagles are scarce and hard to catch. But each fall, for about six to ten weeks, hundreds of bald eagles gather in Glacier National Park in Montana to feed on salmon in McDonald Creek. Here, with so many hungry eagles concentrated in one place, scientists can capture them, attach radio transmitters and wing tags, and let them go. Then the birds can be tracked for the rest of the year, long after they have left the park.

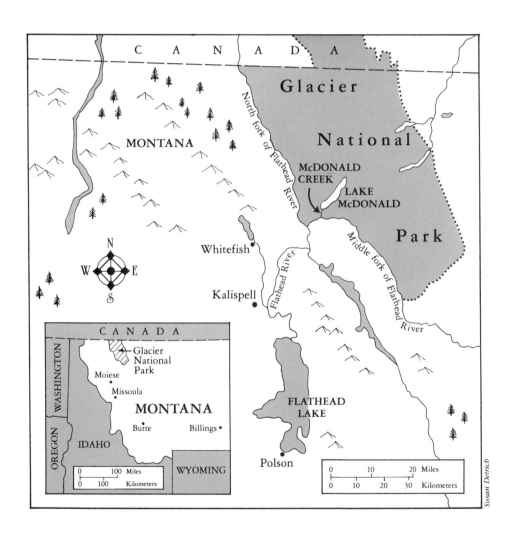

A GATHERING OF EAGLES

The history of the Glacier National Park eagles began in 1916, when the first kokanee salmon were introduced into Flathead Lake, about sixty miles downstream from McDonald Creek. Salmon spawn (mate and release eggs and sperm) in shallow creeks, and some of the salmon in Flathead Lake developed the habit of swimming up to McDonald Creek to spawn. Each female fish lays about five hundred eggs in a nest she scoops from the gravel in the shallow, cold water. The male fish swims along with her and releases sperm to fertilize her eggs as she lays them. After spawning, the adult fish become weaker and weaker and die within three weeks. The young hatch late in March and swim down the creek into the Flathead River and then to Flathead Lake. After four years of growing, the salmon

weigh up to a pound and are ready themselves to swim up to McDonald Creek to spawn and die.

As many as 150,000 fish make the trip each year. Some stop before reaching McDonald Creek and spawn in the shallows of the Flathead River, but most continue up into the creek. Starting in 1939, people began to notice that bald eagles gathered in the park in the McDonald Creek area. Before the 1960s, casual counts of the birds recorded fewer than a hundred each fall. But in the early 1960s, over a hundred birds were seen at one time.

Since 1965, a careful eagle count has been carried out every week once the birds begin to arrive in late September or early October. That year, the maximum number of eagles counted in one day was 189. As the years went by, more and more eagles came. By the mid-1970s, over 300 birds were there at one time, and in the late seventies and early eighties, sometimes over 600 birds were present at a given time. Usually, November is the biggest month for the eagles. By December, the fish are almost gone, and the eagles leave for their winter homes.

This is the Flathead River. Kokanee salmon from Flathead Lake swim through here to get to McDonald Creek, where they spawn.

Opposite: *McDonald Creek is peaceful before the eagles arrive.*
Above: *Early in the morning, once a week, scientists travel the creek in a canoe to count the eagles.*

Glacier National Park is not only a good place for scientists to observe bald eagles, it is also a wonderful place for anyone to see these impressive birds in action. The park is very peaceful in the fall, and there is little sign of activity. The road leading to the eagle's banquet is like a tunnel lined with close-standing birch and pine trees. Only a small sign announces where to go to see the birds, and all is quiet. A short path through woods leads from the parking lot to Apgar Bridge, which stretches across McDonald Creek. Halfway from the lot to the bridge, the path opens into a clearing, suddenly revealing the first clue that something is happening. The strange, piercing cries of eagles fill the air, and birds soar overhead. People on the bridge stare intently toward the creek. The trees by the creek seem studded with white snowballs, but they aren't snowballs at all—they are the heads of dozens of bald eagles resting in the branches.

Below: *People watch the eagles from Apgar Bridge.* Opposite: *How many eagles can you see in this photo taken from Apgar Bridge? The white heads of adult birds are easier to spot than the dark heads of young ones.*

The eagles in the far-off trees are easier to see with binoculars or a closeup camera lens.

Apgar Bridge provides a front row seat to watch bald eagles in action. The water by the bridge is shallow, making a perfect fishing hole for the eagles, and the many trees nearby provide a variety of perches for them to rest and feed. People can watch the birds from the bridge without disturbing them, which is very important. Bald eagles have few natural enemies, but they are wary of humans. Although many salmon spawn in the Flathead River itself, eagles don't hunt there much. People crowd the river's shores catching salmon, and the birds avoid them.

The full-grown kokanee salmon weighs up to a pound.

The eagles will only fish where they can keep a safe distance from people. Loud sounds also unsettle them; a sonic boom will send fifty or more birds skyward. The observers on the bridge show respect for the birds and speak softly so as not to upset them, and the eagles are able to fish and feed in peace close to the bridge.

When an eagle spots a fish close to the water's surface, it flies from its perch. For a moment, the bird is suspended in the air, with its wings spread out over the creek. Then it tilts its tail and dives downward. As the eagle whizzes closer to the fish, it thrusts its feet forward with outstretched talons. When it reaches its prey, it flings its toes downward onto the fish, tightening its grasp and piercing the fish with the sharp talons. Then the bird flies up to a nearby branch to feast on its catch. Often after landing, an eagle will stretch its head upward and let out a series of sharp cries, as if to announce its success.

Above: *Just before catching a fish, the eagle reaches forward with outstretched talons.* Below: *Then it grabs the fish with its claws.*

Above: *The bird flies off with the fish grasped firmly between its feet.* Below: *As the eagle lands, other birds eye its catch.*

Above: *Resting on the branch, the eagle lifts its head and lets out a long, warbling cry.* Below: *Then it settles down to feed.*

The eagle feeds using its powerful pointed beak. The bird takes its time once it has captured a meal, tearing small bites from the carcass until it is finished. Most of the fishing takes place in the early morning and late afternoon hours, with the birds resting quietly in the trees between meals. One eagle may eat four to six fish in a day.

The fall air is cold, but the bird's feathers keep it warm. The feathers can be fluffed up to trap warm air next to the bird's body. Sometimes when an eagle catches a fish, some of its feathers get wet. But the feathers dry off quickly, for they are coated with oil, which keeps water from soaking them. Often, as an eagle rests in the tree, it "preens" itself. It rubs its beak against a special oil gland near its tail. Then it rubs the oil over its feathers.

The bird on the left is a young bald eagle. It lacks the white head and tail feathers of the adult next to it.

Not all the eagles have white heads and tails. Many of them are dark brown all over, while others have patches of white feathers here and there. Their beaks and eyes are also often brown. These birds are young bald eagles. They will not grow the white head and tail feathers until they are four or five years old.

While adult birds can catch live fish, the younger eagles rely mostly on dead fish, which they wade into the creek to get. The development of fishing skills takes several years, and young birds rarely are successful in their at-

Two adult eagles join a young bird in feeding the easy way, on fish that die in the creek after spawning.

tempts to catch fish on the wing. The youngest eagles, which were hatched in the spring, have been out of the nest only about eight to ten weeks when they arrive at Glacier National Park. They have a hard time getting used to feeding themselves. Often, one of these young birds will approach an adult and try to beg for food like a baby in the nest. The adult birds ignore these requests. Life is hard for the young eagles. But if they can live through their first few winters and become wise hunters, they may survive to be forty years old.

LEARNING ABOUT EAGLES

Where do all the eagles in Glacier National Park come from? Only a few pairs nest there during the summer. And where do they go to spend the winter? The only way to find these things out is to follow tagged birds and those with radio transmitters attached to them.

During the fall gathering at Glacier, scientists are busy capturing and tagging eagles. The birds are caught in carefully padded devices baited with dead fish, which are placed in the water. When an eagle wades out to eat the fish, its toe is gently caught. A watching scientist then comes out of hiding and carefully removes the bird. The eagles are calm and do not appear to be upset about being caught.

Before being tagged, a captured eagle is gently wrapped to keep it warm. A leather hood is placed over its head to help calm it.

After capture, the eagle is taken to a quiet place nearby. Its wings are tied down with cloth so it cannot struggle free. A leather hood is put over its eyes. When a bird cannot see, it keeps quiet more easily than when it can see. The sharp talons are placed in a leather bag so they cannot injure the scientists. The bird is wrapped in a blanket to keep it warm.

Each trapped bird has many measurements taken of it. Male and female eagles look almost the same. One of the few ways to tell if a bird is a male or a female is to measure its beak, for females have bigger beaks than do males. The eagle is also weighed and its wingspan is measured. The scientists feel along its breastbone to see how fat it is.

By looking at the color of the eagle's eyes and beak, they can guess about how old an immature bird is. If the beak and eyes are brown, the bird is one or two years old. But if they are lighter in color, on their way to turning yellow, the scientists then know the bird is three or four years old. Whenever the scientists touch the bird, they are very quiet and gentle. This keeps it calm.

Numbered plastic wing markers are put on each bird. They are brightly colored so they can be easily seen. In 1981, for example, orange markers were used on birds

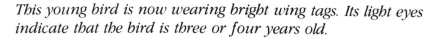

This young bird is now wearing bright wing tags. Its light eyes indicate that the bird is three or four years old.

tagged in Glacier Park. Different colors were used in other places in North America where eagles gather. A few of the birds also are equipped with radio transmitters.

The radio transmitter is fastened with care to the top or bottom of the tail. It is tied on to the strong middle tail feathers. The transmitter has a wire "tail," which is its antenna. The antenna is carefully tied and glued along the middle tail feathers and hangs out a few inches beyond the tail. The bird acts as if the antenna is a very long feather, preening it just as if it belonged.

The antenna of the radio transmitter is carefully fastened to the eagle's tail feathers.

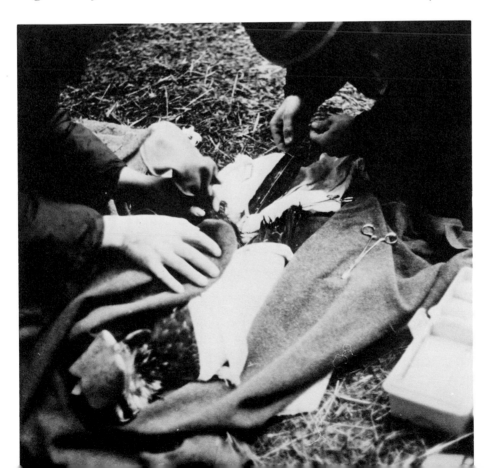

After all the measurements are taken and the trans- mitter is in place, the bird is carried gently back to the creek and released. The wing tags and radio transmitter are very light in weight, and the bird has no trouble get- ting used to them. Once it is freed, the eagle returns to catching fish and fattening up for the winter. But now the scientists know which bird it is. They know how old it is and how much it weighed. They know when it was in Glacier Park. They can follow it and see where it goes when it leaves the park.

A special receiver is used to locate birds with trans- mitters. The receiver can be carried along the ground or taken up into an airplane. Each transmitter gives out its own special beeping signal at a different frequency. The scientist can adjust the receiver to pick up these frequencies so that he or she knows which eagle is being tracked. When the receiver picks up the signal from a bird, the tracker hears the beeping through a set of earphones. The closer to the eagle, the louder the sound. Using the receiver, the scien- tist can track the eagle to its exact location.

Leonard Young, one of the scientists studying the Glacier Park eagles, tracks birds using a receiver and a small antenna.

WHAT WE KNOW NOW

Scientists have been tagging the Glacier eagles since 1977. In 1979, they began equipping the birds with radio transmitters. Already, much has been learned about them. The birds that visit Glacier may stay for only a few days, or they may remain for several weeks. Just how long they stay seems to depend on how abundant the fish are. The fish the eagles eat are very important to their winter survival.

A bald eagle needs about a pound of food (one or two salmon) each day to maintain its weight. But at Glacier, an eagle can get a half dozen fish a day. The birds gain weight rapidly, storing energy for the rest of their winter migration. The feast of fish is especially vital to young eagles, which have been on their own for only several weeks. They can wade into the water to snag the weak and dying salmon. In this way, they get food even though they don't have the finely tuned hunting skills of the adults.

Above left: *This eagle has snagged a dead salmon.* Above right,
below left: *It struggles to shore.* Below right: *On shore, it pauses.*

Above: *Now the eagle begins to eat its salmon.* Below: *But after a short time, the bird flies off with its catch to feed elsewhere.*

Scientists are studying the fish as well as the birds. They hope to understand what the salmon need for successful spawning and for proper growth to maturity. Then officials can try to provide the salmon with the living conditions they need to thrive, so that there will always be a plentiful source of food for the eagles (and fishermen). Unfortunately, there are problems for the salmon. The water level in the Flathead River and in Flathead Lake changes because of dams built to produce electric power. A few years ago, low water levels in winter allowed the eggs of salmon that spawned in the Flathead River to dry out and die. The effects of changed water levels one year showed up four years later when fewer salmon returned to spawn. Because there were less salmon to make the journey up the river, less food was available for the eagles.

The fish face other difficulties, too. One of these involves a shrimplike animal, called the opossum shrimp, which has been found recently in Flathead Lake. In other lakes where this creature lives, it eats up food needed by the salmon, and the fish starve. Although opossum shrimp are still rare in Flathead Lake, the same thing could happen to the salmon there if the number of opossum shrimp increased greatly.

Scientists and the federal and Montana state governments are now cooperating to keep the Flathead salmon population up, for many of the bald eagles in North America count on these fish for food. Today, water levels in the

lake and river are controlled so the salmon eggs are not killed. Human fishing for salmon is also carefully regulated. Scientists expect the fish population to recover by the early 1990s.

The bald eagle is a great traveler. An eagle that is ready to move on from Glacier usually departs in the afternoon, soaring up on the autumn breezes and heading southward down the Flathead River. Sometimes many leave about the same time on the same day. The eagles follow the moun-

Ducks as well as the eagles feed on the dying salmon.

tain valleys as they continue their journey. A few birds spend the winter in western Montana, but most keep moving south. Along the way, the eagles settle in different places for the winter, with certain areas of abundant food serving as key stopovers. While they are in Glacier, the bald eagles do not attack the ducks that share McDonald Creek with them. But during their winter travels, the eagles at times feed on water birds. Sometimes they catch them alive, but they also eat ducks that die from disease or wounds caused by hunters.

Many of the Glacier eagles make their winter homes in the Rush Valley in Utah. Here, a hundred eagles may roost together at night in a single stand of cottonwood trees, feeding by day on the abundant jackrabbits in the area. Other birds, such as hawks and crows, join the eagles in the trees. A few of the Glacier eagles travel farther south or west. Some end up in Oregon, while others journey as far as the Nevada edge of California. This is 750 miles away from Glacier Park.

In March, the eagles begin their northerly migration. While the birds travel hundreds of miles from Glacier to spend the winter, their spring trips involve even more impressive distances. During fall, the birds take time off in Glacier and other places to feed as they move south. But in the spring, the adult birds must hurry to reach their summer homes and start their families, so they move steadily northward. They may fly as far as two hundred miles in

Bald eagles build very big nests high in the treetops.

a day and usually don't stop in one place for very long. Young birds are in less of a hurry than their elders, so they don't fly north as soon. Instead, they may linger where a food source, such as ground squirrels, is abundant.

The eagles travel north past Glacier Park, flying on the eastern side of the Rocky Mountains. On and on they go, through the Canadian province of Alberta, all the way to the shores of Great Bear Lake and Great Slave Lake in the Northwest Territories. Here the birds stop, the adults meeting up with their mates to raise families. Bald eagles mate for life and return to the same area each spring. The birds use the same nests over and over, too, for the giant structures take a long time to build. An eagle's nest may be eight or nine feet wide, twenty feet deep, and weigh as much as two tons. They need to be large, for they become exercise platforms for the young birds when they are old enough to learn to fly.

Scientists are eager to learn just how successful the adult bald eagles are at raising families for bald eagles are

You can see the radio transmitter on top of the tail of this tagged adult eagle.

quite rare. Birds with radio transmitters can be tracked to their nesting areas and observed, to see if they are raising chicks successfully. But catching the adults to put transmitters on them is not easy. They are wise and suspicious. They rarely wade in to take the bait at Glacier, so the scientists are lucky to capture and tag even a few adult birds. One year, when seventy-one birds were trapped, only three were adults. What little has been learned about the nesting success of the Glacier eagles is not encouraging. In a year when six adult birds were given transmitters, five of them paired with mates. Three of these pairs nested, but only one of the nesting pairs actually raised young eaglets. This sounds discouraging, but eagles nesting in some areas have better luck. In Washington, for example, bald eagles nest successfully every year. And in southeastern Alaska, about three thousand pairs of bald eagles raise families along the coast, where there is little disturbance from humans and plenty of fish.

One magnificent eagle lands just as another takes off.

THE ENDANGERED EAGLE

Once bald eagles could be seen in every state except Hawaii. But today this magnificent bird is an endangered species in forty-three states and a threatened species in five. Parts of Alaska and Canada are now the only homes for thriving populations of bald eagles. There are many reasons for this unfortunate loss. Eagles must have peace and quiet to raise their families. Except for the few birds that nest in the treeless far north, where they use cliff or island sites, bald eagles need big old trees for their heavy nests. But much of the old-growth forests that eagles require have been cut down for lumber or replaced by towns and vacation homes.

Poisons have also hurt eagles. Before the pesticide DDT was outlawed, bald eagles and other hunting birds began to disappear. Scientists found that DDT collected in the birds' bodies, making them lay eggs with thin shells that cracked. Now that DDT is no longer used in the United States, some eagles are raising their young successfully. But because of the DDT, and because so much of their habitat has been destroyed, there are many fewer birds of prey now than there used to be.

Eagles also die from other human activities. They are frequently electrocuted by power lines. However, many electric companies are now working with scientists to make power lines and poles safe for eagles.

Some people kill eagles for their feathers. Indians use eagle feathers for their traditional ceremonies. Non-Indians also value eagle feathers and are willing to pay a lot of money for them. But no one can legally kill eagles to get them. A single eagle feather is worth from $10 up, while a whole tail can sell for $450. These high prices attract some people to areas where eagles gather in large numbers, to kill the birds illegally for profit.

In states where animals are trapped for furs, eagles may be attracted to the bait in a trap and get caught. Because eagles hunt by sight, they are only attracted to traps set in the open. In many states, traps must be placed out of sight so that eagles will not find them. But in other states, such as Montana, traps are allowed in the open, and eagles are hurt. When a steel trap snaps shut on an eagle's foot, it can break bones and cut the skin. Injured birds' feet take

One foot of this unfortunate eagle shows the wound and swollen toes of a bird accidently caught in a steel trap set to capture fur animals.

a long time to heal. Because eagles use their feet to capture their food, an injured bird can starve to death before its foot heals.

Unfortunately, many people have mistaken ideas about eagles and think that they are harmful animals. Both bald and golden eagles may feed on dead animals killed by other causes. And occasionally, golden eagles kill young lambs. For these reasons, many ranchers believe that all eagles are a serious danger to their livestock. Some ranchers hate eagles enough to shoot them, even though it is against the law.

These two eagles must remain captives, dependent upon humans for their survival, for they both suffer from broken wings.

Once an Oregon rancher made the mistake of shooting one of the eagles from Glacier Park. After killing the bird, he took off her orange wing markers. But he didn't notice the small radio transmitter under her tail. The young bird, nicknamed Patience, had flown more than five hundred miles from Glacier and had been tracked all along the way. When the radio signal from her transmitter stopped moving, scientists traced it to a rubbish heap on the rancher's land. He confessed to shooting the bird, thinking she was a danger to his livestock. He was fined $2,500 for his crime, which resulted in the loss of a valuable source of information as well as the death of a healthy young eagle.

The bald eagle is valued as a symbol of freedom. But it is special for another reason. The bald eagle is the American national bird. It was chosen for this honor in 1782, when it was used as the central figure in the official national seal. Originally, the seal's designer drew in the golden eagle. But since the golden eagle lives in Europe as well as America, the uniquely American bald eagle was used instead. Ever since, this powerful hunter has captured the imagination of politicians and citizens alike. It appears on the emblems of twelve states and is used as the symbol of many companies and organizations across the country.

Left: *As our national symbol, the bald eagle appears on the Great Seal of the United States.* Right: *The Boy Scouts of America use the bald eagle as a symbol of excellence.*

Despite the popular appeal of the bald eagle, some early politicians were unhappy with its selection as an American symbol. Benjamin Franklin, for example, preferred the wild turkey. Some of the comments made at the time showed attitudes about the bald eagle that still exist today. Franklin criticized the bird as having "bad moral character" and as being "lazy." He said this because bald eagles sometimes steal fish captured by other birds. The famous naturalist John James Audubon thought of the eagle as somewhat of a bully because of its behavior toward other birds. He described it as having a bad temper and thus not being "a model of nobility" for our nation.

Such descriptions of animals as being "bad" or "good" because of their way of life were once commonly made, even by naturalists like Audubon. But today scientists and many others understand that it makes no sense to judge animals as we would people. Each species has its place in the scheme of things, and every living thing has its own right to exist.

Humans can help or harm other forms of life. When we cut down a forest, we kill other plants and animals as well as trees. When we build a dam, we destroy the homes of many kinds of life. When we set aside a wilderness area, we protect the plants and animals that live there. It is important for us to understand the power we have over the lives of other living things and to use it wisely.

Author's Update, 1989

Much has happened to the Glacier National Park eagles since *Where the Bald Eagles Gather* was written. The worst fear of wildlife biologists came true—the salmon population of Flathead Lake collapsed as the number of opossum shrimp soared. Other causes may have also contributed to the salmon's decline. Spawning areas were damaged by the operations of dams upriver, and too many salmon may have been caught by ice fishermen during the wintertime. With fewer fish to eat, the eagles, by 1987, stopped by McDonald Creek only briefly before trying to find food elsewhere. Some congregated in different places where salmon spawn. Others migrated southward to the Swan Valley, where the overabundant deer are frequently killed by automobiles. The dead deer provide an easy food source, especially for the young birds, but at a price. The eagles become so full of food that they must fly down the highway, the only clearing in the woods, to get up speed. As they slowly gain altitude, they often collide with cars coming down the road. The injured birds are taken to wildlife rehabilitators, who nurse them back to health. Unfortunately, some of these eagles do not recover from their injuries well enough to be released again into the wild.

There is some hope for the Flathead Kokanee salmon fishery, however. The populations of whitefish and lake trout in Flathead Lake have increased greatly, while the opossum shrimp have declined. These other fish seem to be feeding on the shrimp. If so, and if they can keep the shrimp population down, the salmon population may recover, and the eagles may one day gather at McDonald Creek to feast again.

INDEX

Page numbers in *italics* refer to captions.